Goodbye Beloved World

Goodbye Beloved World

Scott McCallum

Fintra Publications

© 1969 Scott McCallum
First Published in Great Britain by
Fintra Publications
Distributed through B.D.L.
Iliffe House, Iliffe Avenue,
Oadby, Leicester

218 51547 2

Printed in Great Britain by
Butler & Tanner Limited,
Frome and London

Goodbye Beloved World

I

There was a man called Jonah.

The only difference is that he was a prophet and a holy man, whereas this one is a lay-about.

They were self-indulgent and had got above themselves. So look around you.

Not then; but now. After two thousand years of Christianity. And where do we go from here?

God did not destroy them, as he destroyed Sodom and Gomorrah.

He will not destroy us either. No; He will allow us to destroy ourselves.

But God is dead. I almost forgot.

And there is Science instead, and Technology, and the Universe.

Yes, the Universe. And we are very small beer beside it.

For how could anyone be so ridiculous as to think this little fragment to be the centre of the Universe? It is so big, so immense; and we are so small. Though, by dint of Progress, we have begun to explore it;

And maybe, one day, we shall find another race of little people like ourselves.

What is certain is that we shall never find God.

For that is an old wives' tale, and He is dead.

It is an awful pity. Because with Him everything fell into place.

An ever-lasting and almighty Father who strewed the heavens with the baubles of his constellations,

Who bedecked and illumined the night for the apples of His eye,

And gave us this little sapphire-coloured world of never-ending marvels

Instead of the barren spaces of the moon and the dark inter-stellar cold.

But the wise ones crow ha-ha and say what about cancer and even the cold in the head?

(Forgetting all about miracles like their own stupid little selves)

And if you talk about the Fall, they say oh yes, and doesn't that come just before the Winter?

And then they laugh their silly heads off altogether,

Because, of course, the Fall is an even bigger fable.

And so, dear folks, the biggest laugh of all is waiting for them just round the corner.

For children, and especially wicked children, love a great big bang.

And this, believe me, is going to be the Queen-bee of a Bang.

The Bang, as they say, to end all bangs,

And also, good people, to end our lovely little world,

Now and forevermore. Amen.
And if you don't believe me,
Or even if you do,
Just read on.

II

Yes, the other night I was standing on the Western
    European seaboard.
It was a bay. The sky was full of stars.
But on the other side there were the motor head-
    lamps,
All chasing each other,
And so unable to see the stars.
We cannot see the stars for Progress.
I said this to my dog,
A big golden dog, enjoying the night odours.
And he looked at me with calm, affectionate eyes,
So that I stroked his ear.
—Are there any dogs on the moon?
Don't be so bloody stupid.

You think that nonsense?
Maybe you don't care for dogs anyway.
What do you care for? Maybe sex?
Is there any sex on the Moon?
No, it's all being used up on the Earth.
I ask you.
Do you want to sell a watch?
Or a cement-mixer?
Pour in one navel, two hips, and a torso,
Shake them well and dish up hot.
Not that I dislike the female form;
Just exactly on the contrary.
For beings with our kind of built-in criteria,
It's wonderful.
In fact that is the trouble.
It is much too wonderful
To be used for making money
Or for sending the entire human race round the
    bend.
I believe, in fact, it owes all its wonderfulness
To having been constructed by Holy Trinity Inc.
And not by Julius Greenbaum of Hail Columbia,
    Pa.,
Who is convinced of it.
Only one thing I ask of the good Lord:

Why, as well as curves,
He did not endow little dames
With some more cerebral matter
So that they could avoid being used
By certain po-faced citizens
To line their pockets.
When I see them parade around
Like pedigree cattle or organ-monkeys,
I often think that
If cow-pats were proclaimed to be fashionable
 headwear,
No poor old cow's poop would be without its
 queue.
(The pun was not intended.)
Anyway, it is all very sad.
But then, of course, I was wrong about the good
 Lord,
For the really brainless tracts of the female popula-
tion
Became such only when
Instead of being girls and women
They opted to be, precisely, little dames.
We, they, and the world in general, all lost a great
 deal by it.
And do you know something?
Did you ever hear of an old-time hit-number called
 the Apocalypse?
This, believe it or not, was meant as the curtain-
 raiser to the big Bang.

And the individual who pulls the rope in it is called
　　the Beast;
Yes, just like that, the Beast.
That's the only name they give him, but,
And this has been a teaser for whole generations of
　　learned citizens,
He was given a cipher, a Mark.
In this old number, the Apocalypse,
'The Mark of the Beast', it says, 'is six-six-six'.
Now, I admit, of course, that this sounds just like
　　his telephone number,
Or even James Bond.
But, do you know what?
In those days everybody spoke Latin,
Just as today everybody speaks English.
(Well, I know, but some of the Latin wasn't so
　　good either.)
And if you transpose the Latin 6 6 6 into the world-
　　wide language of today,
Do you know what comes out for the Mark of the
　　Beast,
I mean, the prelude to the Big Bang?
Why, strangely enough, dear people, it comes out
　　as Sex-Sex-Sex!
—Which strikes me as being, perhaps whimsical,
But anyway,
Extraordinarily apt.

IV

What was I saying? Ah, yes;
Sex, Sex, Sex!
You see, again, even in a book like this,
One just cannot get away from it.
However, I mentioned Latin.
Now Latin hasn't reeked of sex, has it, for a very
    long time;
Not, I should say, since Ovid.
For what happened to it after that? Why, it became
    converted.
Non angli sed angeli.
Initium Sancti Evangelii
Secundum Johannem
—And all that jazz.
Who said that?
Why, the Pope!
You don't believe me?
Well, you show me some Latin around today.
And the Pope is the head of the Church, is he not?
Oh, how stupid of me,
I almost forgot about Collegiality.
Which means, of course, that
The infallibility of the Pope
Becomes that of the Bishops.
Sorry again, that of the Clergy,

Or should it be, save the mark,
'The People of God'?
I don't know. Do you?
It used to be so simple.
Et in unam sanctam catholicam
From the Faroes to the Falklands
By way of Beachy Head.
But they took out the cement from between the
    bricks,
And the lot fell, not upon Matthias, but upon us.
Who took out this Latin cement and began it all?
The Pope? Or the Bishops?
Or that lousy, stinking minority of presumptuous
    little men
Masquerading as
The People of God?
I don't know.
But again do you want to know something?
Ever hear of a type called Malachy?
This Malachy was an Abbot,
Son of Erin, fluent Latin speaker, who lived
A thousand years ago or so.
In those days, before Electricity or Television,
People passed the time having Visions.
(Some still do, they say, but it's no longer news.)
Anyway, it seems Malachy saw all the Popes
From then to now.
And instead of an Apocalyptic cipher
He gave them each a phrase,

(No, not the kind they use in Portadown)
Something characteristic of the man,
His epoch, his life, his birthplace,
Or even, as we are forced to believe
In the present instance,
His coat of arms.
Pacelli's label we all know about,
Because they made a film on him
And called it just specifically that,
Pastor Angelicus.
I thought it highly suitable.
Not to speak of poor old Benedict the Fifteenth
Who happily reigned, as the saying goes,
During the first World War.
Religio Depopulata, said Malachy,
Or in the present-day vernacular,
Religion Laid Waste.
For the cataclysm above-mentioned,
For the rise of World Communism
And of Materialistic Atheism,
Not bad picking, folks,
Not bad at all, considering
The obvious lack of form.
Could only be inside information, I should say,
Straight from the Stable, so to speak;
And that is bad, because
This Irish ecclesiastical tipster
Who, speaking all these centuries ago,
Described the epoch of the next one as

De Medietate Lunae
Thus, it seems to me, scoring another bull
(Possibly with a moon-shot in reverse)
And anyhow being bang up-to-date,
Foresaw only three more Popes to go
Before the last of all
Petrus Romanus
And the Big Bang.
Good people, work it out for yourselves.
None of us asked to be born Catholic or Jew,
Cape-coloured, or a dweller on the Yang-tze
    River;
All of us are drawn to our inherited philosophies,
And each will be judged according to his lights;
Yet truth exists on earth, not just subjective truth,
And what's stood firm, like the proverbial Rock,
All through the tempests, earthquakes, and erup-
    tions
Since Augustus reigning and the world at peace?
Why, only one great Fortress, one alone;
And if you don't believe me, read Macaulay
Who said it most compellingly.
This was the basis and the bastion
That made the mighty, truth-revealing West,
The splendid Hebrew–Graeco-Christian West,
And even that of General Custer.
But anyhow this rock-like Fortress
Was built to stand against
Any and all attack,

Save sapping from within, the inside job.
When garrison command begins itself
To lay the charges against truth,
Then, I ask you,
If you were the Supreme Commander,
What would you do?—I think I know.
Shorten lines, and write it all off.
Dies irae, dies illa,
Solvet saeclum in favilla.
Uh-huh. That's just another, more traditional way
   of saying
The Big Bang.
All for a little bit of apostolic, universal Latin?
Not quite; more for a vast presumption;
Not pride of Lucifer,
But mealy-mouthed presumption,
Ecclesiastical Socialism.
And let me end by saying
That any four thousand bishops
Or four hundred thousand priests
Who gutlessly abandon
Their *Introibo*'s and their plainsong *Credo*'s
Distilled for them in monastery cells,
In cloister and cathedral,
Through hours and seasons,
Years and centuries of holy dedication,
Are in my opinion
To this extent
And always humanly speaking

Not worth a damn.
And never let it be forgotten, dearly beloved folks,
It is not lively ladies
Or income-tax inspectors
That the Lord doth vomit
Out of His mouth.
Oh no, it is the lukewarm, you remember,
The boys who run
Exclusively on the spot
By, for instance, plugging the New Liturgy;
Who to fables turn
(*Ad fabulas autem convertentur*)
Who favour Catechisms
In double-Dutch,
—And all that jazz.
These are the characters, you mark my words,
That God will surely vomit out of His mouth,
And make an end.

V

And did I mention, I think I did,
Ecclesiastical Socialism?
Well, that, of course,—you ask Pope Paul—
Merely reflects the lay variety.
And that, again, means Politics.
So, who killed Kennedy anyway?
Nobody knows,
Excepting you and I and the whole American
    people.
And who killed sixteen other folk as well,
Just one at a time,
For being too curious?
And who killed Bobby?
Why, naturally, the Kuwait Sheiks
Or the Desert Song
Or something else out of the Arabian Nights.
It stands to reason, does it not?
I mean, the Middle East.
Of course it does; and anyhow
The case is closed;
The Dallas Sheriff said it.
And doctors knew, right from the start,
That Ruby, poor old boy, had cancer.
Oh say, have you seen?
I have indeed.

But where fares it better?
Perhaps in England's green and pleasant land,
Or, possibly, among the Market Six?
Like hell it doth.
For Europe's sick to death.
Around her bier
Stand long-nosed Charles,
Harold the Unsteady,
And, let's say, Fanfani.
A pretty deadly crew, by God.
Shades of Thermopylae and Roncevaux,
The great Renaissance and the City States,
Shades of Runnymede and Thomas More,
Shades of a myriad glowing things.
They're all shades now, from Pericles to
    Churchill.
And who killed Cock-Robin?
Why, partly Marx, who cut the head
From off the body politic;
Partly Trades Unions, who all eat their tails
And trample on their mothers;
Partly the Wars, some greed, much lust;
But anyhow, Cock Europe's dead,
And that is that.
This Europe that has filled the world
With Poetry and Art and wise Philosophy,
Dance and Provençal song and sunburnt mirth,
Shakespeare and Johnnie Walker,
It's gone; dead by its own fell claw.

With Europe dead, who wants to live?
Not me.
Much though one may admire
The cosmic flea-hops of the Astronauts
And Japanese transistors,
Man doth not live alone
By higher plumbing.
But there are other places on our planet, are there
    not?
Roll up and take a look—
Ah, woe is me, I have to say it—
At Europe's shame.
So small a thing, some pigment in the skin,
To blind one to one's brother.
Learie Constantine (that's Gary Sobers's prede-
    cessor)
Once bowled a mighty fast one.
For Learie said the following:
The white man came, said Learie,
And finding us in highly barbarous surroundings,
Gave us the Bible;
Now the whole thing's changed, said he,
For we have got the Bible,
And he, poor chap, owns all the barbarous sur-
    roundings.
A very fast one.
Well, what's the answer?
The monks and missionaries who produced the
    Book

Were not the gents who did the property develop-
ment?
All very true; but the fact that these olden-time
developers
Sent wife and daughter primly out to church,
And that eventually their sons fetched up in Eton,
Makes it all highly complicated.
So brood a space on Africa, on Asia, and even Latin
America.
Consider the devil's parody of China and the
Russian glass-house,
Where but to think, to say it once again with
Keats,
Is to be full of sorrow
And leaden-eyed despairs.
Look around your world, God's world.
The West be-sotted, undermined, the East en-
slaved,
And not a principle in sight,
Not a belief,
From which to start again.
After two thousand years?
No, no, dear reader; work it out.
You must, I think, agree with me;
It's all been said.
All save one little word,
One little, final, tiny, tired word,
—Goodnight.

⌘ VI ⌘

Bit heavy going, maybe. Let's have some relaxa-
    tion,
A whiff of comic relief, light entertainment.
Right then, led on by Learie, here's a jingle
That we used to know:
'It's not for the sake of a ribboned coat,
Or the empty joy of a season's fame'—
—You bet it's not; bring out the Bentley, boy!
That's sport I'm talking of;
At which you will remark
'Come off it, George.
Don't tell me that the world is going to end
All because Wimbledon has gone professional?'
That's it, dear brother, more or less that's it.
The spirit's gone, transmogrified itself to L.S.D.
And counting medals.
It all began
By going round the golf-course with a putter,
The craze for records, all of which need time,
And time is money.
So what's the score today?
Italians buy the referee and doctor urine; whereas
In Argentine they spit;
Whilst England's sporting youths, tough as their
    sires,

Slay dragons in the shape of British Rail,
And any day will tease the toilet-paper.
But surely, one protests, the spirit still descends
With flights of amateurs all lily-white from high
  Olympus?
It does, dear brother, but last time, I much regret
  to say,
It did the snowy slopes on heated runners;
Whilst once upon the flat, the great Phidippides
Donned one black glove;
And other heroes wore across their chests
Such strange devices as
What-you-may-call-em's Pills for Flatulence
Or, Sprint with Castor.
Do you, then, take my point?
All the fair things in life are fouled beyond recall,
Like booting of a ball around a field for love of it
Or even, if you so prefer, just for the hell of it.
And should you think this nothing,
Why then, O foolish man,
Nothing's the sum of all your little wisdom,
And the Bang's too good for you.

It may be you will think of the above: it is not
    serious.
Alright; let's find a subject which most definitely
    is, like, say,
The world we are preparing for tomorrow, if it
    comes,
The youths and blushing maidens of today.
Two lovely words: the youths and maidens.
How sad there are no more of them around;
Because, of course, there aren't;
And should you ask where have they gone,
    alack,
The answer is
They gave up measles for the death-wish.
A thing which, after all, is not too hard to under-
    stand;
Because, if everyone is held stone-cold at twenty-
    seven,
The only reasonable answer, anticipating this,
Is suicide, obviously, at twenty-three.
Don't you agree?
Once you proclaim that youth is king and sage,
The eye among the very blind indeed,
The only thing a chap can do, with any
    decency,

Is clear the stage for those apprentice sorcerers aged
   twelve,
Now climbing into costume in the wings.
O wondrous age,
Where life begins at twelve, or maybe ten, and
   from then on
One knows just everything by being young.
O miracle of rare device,
O blessed Progress.
To know it all, and then to cease to know,
Upon the midnight, or some sunny afternoon, at
   twenty-three.
Mind you, don't get me wrong, I realise quite well
That one will still absorb regurgitations
From Oracle-Computers and High-Priestly Plum-
   bers,
And will continue, for what time remains,
To occupy a place around the house;
So that one's epitaph should one day be
They buried him at ninety who died at twenty-
   three.
But let's forget it;
Youth is for now, life is for lotusing,
And since so short, must all be drained and dregged,
Till sated and be-scuppered,
Drugged and draggled,
Abdicating from omniscience, at twenty-three,
One passes on the torch, or buck,
And gets, symbolically, one's hair cut.

Yes; it's a hairy spectacle alright.
You see, I always did love youth, even when
    young;
And still today am moved by its defencelessness.
What shower of blackguards turned the whole
    world upside-down?
Only two, old friend;
Two formidable characters, with names most
    quaint,
Undoubtedly the Yellow Peril, or something such,
Two gents, in any case, responding to the oriental
    monikers
Of Hi Yoo and Wot Mee.

VIII

Is it possible? Yes, I'm afraid it is.
And if, of this litany of accusation wailing around
  us,
You would hear some part,
Perpend.

✤ IX ✤

There used to be a very witty tale which said
That in a New York cemetery
There stood a monument thus propagandistically
  inscribed:
Here lies no one, because they used our contra-
  ceptives.
A real side-splitter.
Yes, poor youth who do not exist, we suppressed
  you.
Your father's strong protective arm
Pushed you back into oblivion.
Your mother's loving breasts had other, more
  aesthetic uses.
With selfish hearts we opted for our fun,
Only our fun;
Regretfully we took the Pill,
Or crushed your tiny skull,
—All legally, of course; all clean and clinical;
For what's a curly head, you understand,
Beside the Joneses?

Still, son, or maybe infant daughter,
We did have other babes;
Few, you know, and nicely spaced.
They started well; smiling, clear-eyed,
Whose goo-goo prattle strewed our path with
  roses.
And then? Well then, you know, we orphaned
  them.
Incompatibility it was; or George, or Aimée;
Anyhow, our fun.
Yes, I'm afraid we made some other little shades,
Who wept their hearts out, in bitter childish
  solitude,
And learned their fondness, trueness and morality
From seeing Mummy climbing into bed
With Daddy's oldest friend,
Before graduating to the milkman.

ᘓᕼᕲᘓ XI ᘓᕼᕼᕲᘓ

Some of us stayed together, though; maybe we
  hadn't the guts.
Anyhow, we stayed.
So all was well? Oh no, poor living youth, we
  abdicated.
Things like cheaper female labour, women's rights,
  equality of sex,
Those blasted Joneses and the changing world
All had some hand in it.
The upshot was you lost your mother,
Poor old crumb,
And had to settle for an elder sister;
Not, let me say, the decent kind one once depended
  on,
But something new in multicoloured plastic.
Oh, poor old crumb indeed,
For you and I well know,
O little boy or small forlorn girl,
There is no substitute in all the wide, wide world,
For one, just one, old-fashioned mother.
—Well, I ask you, is there?

XII

Fundamentally, that's it: the root and cause of all
    our evil,
The reason why the world has now to die, lies
    there:
Youth, poor unhappy youth, has lost its mother;
The hand that rocked the cradle's kicked the
    bucket;
And the loss is not just grave, it is irreparable.
I mean, of course, you've lost your father too;
You and your Pop have both today been flung
Upon the desiccated dugs
Of married career-women;
Or else, at best, on bosoms much restricted and
    impaired
By labour Nature never had in mind.
You lost your mother, son; your father too; your
    hearth and home;
And got, instead, mod. cons.
It seems to me a very mod. return.

⌒⌒⌒ XIII ⌒⌒⌒

By contrast, and with no thought, believe me,
Of holier than thou,
I remember going to Midnight Mass last Christmas
In a remote hamlet up in the Swiss mountains.
There still had not been time
For the progressive message to seep through,
And it was all there,
The bells, the Crib, the candles, the expectant
    congregation,
And the *Missa de Angelis;*
We sang it all together.
It was (almost) like that Nearer, my God, to Thee,
Upon the doomed Titanic.
Never mind, we sang it;
And walked home through the falling snow,
Holding our little daughter by the hand,
From her first Midnight Mass.
Maybe that does not say anything to you.
It would, could you have seen her shining eyes,
Fascinated by the beauty,
Transformed by being identified
With the most wondrous tale in all the universe,
In such surroundings.
And were not children sent to us for things like these?
And what's our fun beside them?

Need I, to double-coin a phrase, say more?
Perhaps I'll play the Prisoner's Friend,
Just very briefly,
Stating the older generation's case.
It's only fair:
Childhood and youth, we abandoned you?
Took away Mummy's knee?
Yes, but we offered in return
Two channels (one in colour),
Ulster, Regional, and I.T.V.
We gave you screen and stage to fill your empty
    hours
And prurient curiosities;
You learnt what life was really all about;
Almost, that is; for, possibly due to chronic con-
    stipation,
No one as yet has staged a buskined bowel-move-
    ment;
—It's all there's left to do.—
We loaded you with loot to invest
In sexy magazines, high-circulation papers,
Which showed the world as naught but incest,
    rape,
Murder, and other such-like innocent capers.
All this we gave you;

Plus the Nelson eye to your new-fangled foibles;
Incensed the calf-shrine of your personality.
What more, I ask you, could we do?
Not a damned thing.
Caught as we are in what is jocularly termed
The daily rat-race,
Even the smallest mites must surely come to know
This fully occupies their parents' time, with
    nothing over.
One can only do one's best—
Though, of course, it has to be admitted that some
    things, well,
Just aren't any more around;
Like the old Bible narratives, or knights and
    maidens,
Or even the widow's son, that local boy made
    good,
Who brought her to a castle, with himself and
    princess,
Instead of to the Old Folks' Home alone;
That kind of thing, you know;
But, hell, you can't have everything.
And then, it cannot have escaped your notice,
With cinema and television,
And their own high-powered publications,
Children grow up extraordinarily fast;
My wife and I, in point of fact, just feel
They are extremely capable of looking after them-
    selves;

Which, by and large, is just exactly
What we let them do.
—And so it goes.
The Prisoner's plea, it's clear, is the old classic
Nemo dat quod non habet, which is to say, God wot,
You cannot give to others that which you have
   not got.
And this again is just the point where we came in,
To find youth standing on the stage of life,
Alone, unloved, untutored, left to his own devices,
And therefore devising.
Prisoner stand up; you've had it.
You lack both blood and guts.
You're guilty and condemned to death, by Bang-
   ing,
Justly, if paradoxically, at dawn.
And may the Lord have mercy on our rotten souls,
For we it is, all of us, as previously stated,
Who stand before the Bar.

Anything else? Yes, this.
In palmier adolescent days, those suffering from
The home's inadequacy
Found possible refuge, potential balm,
In education.
To famous men we chanted lauds
In Kipling's spanking chorus,
Who beat the lights from us with rods
For all the love they bore us.
Not much love or rods around nowadays.
Rods are out; love has been replaced by the Wel-
     fare State;
And beyond that lies only the Burnham Scale
Of Salaries and Pensions.
Whilst besides, apart from politicians who by
     definition
Know less and less about more and more
Till they know sweet damn-all about every-
     thing,
Today is an age of increasing specialisation,
Wherein every conscientious tutor's aim must be
To know more and more about less and less
Till he knows all the bleeding lot about nothing.
The poor old Groves of Academe have had their
     day.

Can you believe it? Teaching youngsters only to
    think!
It was not serious; no double-entry, no cash-flow;
No wonder they had to walk.
And so, like other unproductive building areas,
The Groves have gone;
Bulldozed they say; butchered to make
The Massachussetts Institute of Technology.
O Socrates, O Plato, O Aristotle!
Only the parents of Onassis have thought of you
    for ages.
—It's not, you see, that one dislikes
Putting in a coin, as it were,
And maybe getting the answer;
Or getting out the day before one started
At San Francisco;
No, not at all;
But if the price is youth's immortal soul,
The tariff's much too high.
And should you think this is, once more,
Drawing the longish bow,
Then pray expound to me upon the incandescent
    state
Of halls of learning all across the world,
Save Peking and Siberia,
Where ovule-pated Senates, old in command,
Vamoose and seek the quiet desert air,
Whilst rows of shining morning faces,
Nature's abhorred vacuum 'twixt their ears,

Make law, and hay, and merry un-jugged hell.
The answer, actually, is relatively simple.
To dithering bankruptcy and egotistical abdication
From all save self and the cause of material pro-
gress,
Whereby Society, even in its alleged mentors,
Reflects in general the ills of the individual,
Youth responds purely by instinct;
Whereto is added some dash of Comintern
And other sundry bitters.
Just as some animal, destined for slaughter,
Scents its approaching end, and runs amok,
So our unhappy youth feel also that around the
corner
There's grass and water for them, could they but
find it;
Some substitute for parent-teacher owners
By whom they've been abandoned;
So, putting down their heads, they stampede.
After some time, lost in the headiness of smashing
all in sight,
They don't remember what began it all.
And then, instead of clover,
Find themselves ringed around by lethal weapons.
There's no escape.
One way or another, they feel,
The Bang will come.

And so our little victims play,
Bedecked and garlanded by Carnaby Street,
With juke-box flutes and timbrels, not unheard.
They receive the limelight for, as has been said,
There stands tomorrow's world, that world on
  which
The count-down has begun.
Wherefore were they led, one asks again,
To this, the sacrificial launching-pad,
And aimed at nowhere?
Again it has been said: for selfishness and abdication
Multiple in form,
But all with the label Progress.
Might we, perchance, before the final line,
Direct one fleeting, valedictory glance
At this here Progress?
Let's see.

❧ XVII ❧

Guess what I saw the other day:
All the ships in the world tied up,
All the trains too,
And all the people in the world walking to work,
Because some little Union jerk,
Who probably never did a decent day's work in
    his life,
Just happened to feel that way.
It's too much honour to include the louts
In this, the world's sad requiem;
But there they sprawl
Across the sunset of our western world,
The Union leaders.
Never in the history of mankind
Has so much squit
Been poured upon so many by so few.
They victimise us all, person and nation;
Dictate our policies;
And, with their mini-brains,
Ruin our economies;
To benefit of whom?
Of creeds and nations,
Where, even to whisper the word strike
Means sudden death.
I ask you,
Is this, then, Progress?

ʘʘʘ XVIII ʘʘʘ

Do you know what else I saw?
All the policemen in the world tied up
By Left-Wing politicoes;
And highly progressive territories
Where only the thugs were safe,
Only the criminal sure of a warm bed;
Where none but the normal citizen,
His wife and daughter,
Had to be frightened of rope or lead;
And that too, I suppose, is the very acme of Pro-
gress.

Amazing how much Progress you perceive, if you
    just look around you.
Ever read the Financial Times? Skim through the
    City Editors?
Well now, in the name of Adam Smith
And the cornucopia of the Market Basket,
Can anybody tell me how, in times like ours,
Of stream-lined management, instant communica-
    tion,
Automation, exploitation, and planned production,
The world's entire economy seems sick,
And every other currency on crutches?
Are there gnomes, elves, ogres
Bedevilling it all?
I'm only asking. It's a humble question.
But if there are, I would remind them,
Without conviction,
That this time they will all most literally be
Hoist with their own petard;
After which, there is that departure of the damned:
Admirably described by a legendary Scots divine
'Lord, Lord, we didna ken,' they wailed in woe;
And the Lord, with dryness infinite, succinctly said
'Ah, well—ye ken noo!'
A deplorable position for characters so used

To hedging and to forward buying;
The Exchange irrevocably closed, their pants ever-
    lastingly down.
I recommend these pawky lines of Scottish eschato-
    logy
To their progressive, earnest meditation;
—Again, may I say,
Without very much conviction.

Or maybe our universal social ills
Are linked to another peculiar phenomenon,
Whereby, through nationalisation, exorbitant tax-
    ation,
And the monstrous Moloch of estate duty,
All man's creativeness, adventurousness and thrift
Are stifled, together with his freedom and his
    loyalties;
Are progressively held in thrall
By faceless, dull, presumptuous little men,
Who, if constrained to earn a living for themselves,
Would die of exposure.
(Whereas, the wicked capitalist who ceases to
    create,
For himself and for others,
Perforce collapses.)
Could it, do you think, be this?
And is this also Progress?

Or, tell me, do you at times peruse the Sunday
  press?
There's surely Progress with a great large letter P,
At least sixty pages of it,
And no sector of the world missed out.
You remember Three Men in a Boat?
With all the maladies in existence, excepting house-
  maid's knee,
Just walk around me once, he said, and qualify.
Thus with the Sunday papers;
Run through them once, and Progress is yours.
For there you'll learn Picasso still confounds
The left-wing optic with the umbilicum;
Or Henry Moore has whirled another whorl
And called it Soul-Mates.
On Shaftesbury Avenue Hair has given way,
With even more suggestiveness,
To Baldness;
Whilst Sigmund Zeitglock on cinerama
Deserts his flesh-pots of the female epidermis
And starts on homos.
Architecture squares, not only the hypotenuse,
But, *Splendor Ordinis*, everything in sight.
And *Ars Poetica*, calm recollection of emotion,
Appears as neither art nor poesy,

But undiluted ocular lotion.
Music, the heavenly maid, has lost her touch
And takes in washing; though still she strums,
For old time's sake, upon her wash-board.
—The Sunday press, without regard for friends or
   foes,
Sketches our world exactly as it goes.
And if that be indeed the way it goes,
Or doesn't,
If that is Progress,
What can one say, if not to stuff it.
Except that, friend, they'll stuff you too, and me,
And all who love that other world
Which by their negative perversions
They have denied and spat upon.
The good Lord is not vulgar—unlike me;
He'll use another phrase like, say, Get on with it;
Which is to say, that like the well-known Roman
   governor,
He'll wash His hands of us.
The Bang will be, in keeping with our times,
Strictly a Do-it-Yourself job.

Well no; not altogether.
We've had a hand, from one
Formerly listed as Lucifer, the Morning Star.
All dramas have their villain;
That of humanity is no exception.
I mean, of course, the Devil;
Which is the boldest statement made so far,
Inviting irony and ribaldry and flower-pots,
With lots of talk about this day and age.
Let us, however, just define our terms
(Princely predecessor of semantics).
Should the Satanic image be of horns,
Of cloven hooves, and red combinations,
Nego paritatem; that's not my man.
That is the clown the dear old Miracle Plays
Once took the mickey from, and thought it up-
    roarious.
He's made the greatest play of it every since,
To camouflage, no operatic situation,
But a super-duper red-hot Institute of Strategic
    Studies.
The character in question is best described
As the Spirit of Evil.
You know him well; for he it is
Who's always whispering in our ready ear;

And he's the type who's orchestrated
Your evil, mine, and that of all the world,
To make today's presumptuous cacophony.
Tell me, have you ever studied Michelangelo's
    Last Judgment,
Upon the wall of the Sistine Chapel?
The great man did not attempt the Spirit of Evil.
He introduced the classical, and painted Charon
Thudding them on to the ferry.
But right in the middle of the picture
He gave the world's most graphic illustration
Of Satan's handiwork;
The face of a man who absolutely knew
That all was over; that the world had gone,
And there was no return.
One sees his marrow and his blood are frozen
Right into his body
By that unspeakable knowledge.
No other gaze, portrayed by man, has ever held
Such lonely, desperate, hopeless terror.
It's worth a look from all of us,
All of us dealing in flesh and foreign exchange,
All of us destined, like the world, to die.
And it has nothing whatsoever to do with red
    combinations,
But fits in singularly well with the Spirit of Evil.
Should this once more, however, tax your credu-
    lity,
Sweat out the final chapter.

There have been attempts at humour, as they put it,
In these poor pages;
Confitebor Tibi in cithara, Deus, Deus meus;
But nothing, absolutely nothing, was ever more
    serious.
Let me put it to you one last time.
Having considered the world, again let's emphasise
    it,
After two thousand years of Christianity,
Where do we go from here?
Two thirds of the world starving;
Half of the world in slavery;
The rest in chains of its own individual making;
The Church, the seamless garment, sundered from
    top to bottom;
Decency, discipline derided;
Morality not even paid the tribute of immorality
In our permissive times;
Age self-engrossed and abdicated; youth fed to the
    wolves;
Science, swollen with insolence, confounding dis-
    covery of what has always existed
With autonomous creation; not even converted
By the new terrestrial star sighted at Christmastide
By our wise-men astronauts;

Man convinced of starting his observations from
    scratch,
Oblivious to the hypothesis of his own existence,
His reason, senses, organs,
The wonder ready-made and mass-produced
Of all his unique being;
The crass denial of the Intelligence which fashioned
Not only him, but all the unending miracles of
    creation,
The orbits and the rules for orbiting
For all the crude complexities of these our Sputniks
    and Apollos;
And, I repeat, not a conviction or a principle in
    sight
On which to build; after two thousand years;
Years which began when,
The world then too being sick and highly pro-
    gressive,
The Remedy was vouchsafed, the Leaven;
And much indeed was remedied and duly leavened.
The Legionaries' roads became
Paths out of Aquin and Assisi
That left behind them monuments in stone and
    colour,
Symbols and spiritual reflections,
Never surpassed by man.
—Bring out today our brittle little men,
Our Plumbers, extra-sensory philosophers;
Lead on our planners and our speculators;

Take a good look; and then conclude,
Somewhere along the way, we lost it.
We've reached the last dead-end.
Just as our ferro-concrete mole-hills
Shut out the grass, the sunlight, and the sky above,
So have we shut out God, focal point of the picture,
Essential piece whose lack makes senseless all our
    jig-saw puzzles.
We took out God, killed Him, proclaimed Him
    dead;
And God will do just that, stay dead.
Let's take a leaf from Nabuchodonosor's outdoor
    cinema;
The writing's on the wall; I told you so already;
It's called the Apocalypse, where man kills all Man-
    kind.
You see, ever since what's called the dawn of
    history,
Man has been bashing himself with weapons of
    percussion,
The flint, the spear, the high-explosive shell;
Only today can he, quite literally,
Disintegrate himself and all around him.
As the parrot said in the conjuring story,
When the ship's boilers blew up,
That's a very progressive trick indeed; but bloody
    dangerous.
It is.
From the original atom we've progressed

Through hydrogen to cobalt.
With all the clever Plumbers that there are around,
Cobalt by now must be a back number.
Anyhow, one of these days, somebody's going to
press the button,
Drop the test-tube,
Somehow, somewhere set off a chain reaction,
And so to bed.
And if you care to thumb through that old number,
the Apocalypse,
You'll find the stage directions for the Four Horse-
men
All strangely reminiscent of radio-active fall-out;
Whilst some of the stage effects described on land
and sea
Are but the full-scale application
Of our experimental junketings around the
atolls.
No; don't have any doubts; the spectral steeds stand
saddled,
And the old chap with the egg-timer stands
whetting his scythe,
And goes to mow a meadow.
Mind you, if your accounts tot up,
There's no abnormal need for trepidation.
Since that far-off dawn referred to,
The world has ended every day for every man who
died.
This way, we just take off together.

But, on the other hand, no more little wonder-
filled children
Wandering and plucking flowers through this
world of wonders.
—Some time ago, in visiting a painting exhibition,
I came across a canvas where
The artist showed the ancient Stygian realm of
death;
And there among the mournful hooded shades
Stood a small golden-haired girl, a new arrival;
All dressed in white, with short white socks,
And in her hand, precisely, a bunch of wild flowers.
The look of innocence, bewilderment, fear and
aloneness
In the child's eyes, wrung out my innards,
Even though I knew the concept to be false.
'Suffer little children,' it once was said,
'Of such is the kingdom of heaven.'
And, children, if the good Lord does some juggling
with my figures,
And lets me in, then you'll be seeing quite a lot
Of this old stick and Francis Thompson;
For he's the man who wrote
'Look for me in the nurseries of heaven.'
A charming thought.
But anyway, what I wanted to say to you was this:
Don't worry about any old nasty bang;
For you it's summer thunder.
The only world of shades that you could know

Is all the foulness waiting to besmirch you.
Your muted, friendly, dying peal of thunder will
   surely come
Out from a summer cloud;
And a Voice will say to you,
As Thompson once more has it,
'All which I took from thee I did but take
Not for thy harms
But just that thou might'st seek it in My arms.
All which thy child's mistake
Fancies as lost, I have stored for thee at home;
Rise, clasp My hand, and come!'
And, little children, there you will pluck more
   bright and lovely flowers,
You, the finest, the most wonderful works
Of God's creation.
It is tragic there should be so few of you
Left for the world in stock;
But in the circumstances,
Eminently understandable.
Here endeth the lesson.

ᏅᎮᎦᏯ EPILOGUE ᏅᎮᎦᏯ

You may with justice ask, wherefore or why this
    scrappy splurge
In maccaronic prose?
Is it a cry of Bogey-man to make us put things right?
No, it is not; the whole thing's gone too far;
We know it all, you see;
This is the last round up.
The world will end, maybe not today, but cer-
    tainly tomorrow night.
That the human species would eventually check out
Has long been understood, but
No living generation could ever think
It would possibly happen to them.
Remember the trite old phrase The Buck Stops
    Here?
Well, this is Here.
So why, then, bother splurging?
Just the fact that when one's neighbour is about to
    be run down
All of us once were taught it manners to yell Look
    Out.
This is also Look Out.
There's something more.
Do you recall the story of the Soviet farmer, whose
    gnarled hands,

Tops in the whole U.S.S.R.,
Brought him to Moscow?
They said to him, in his conducted tour of Radio
    Building,
Any word spoken within this room is heard
    through all the world.
Christ, said the farmer—H E L P !
And this, again, is——Help!
I mean to say that though the issue, globally, is dead,
Nothing to be done,
There must be other gents
Scattered around the surface of the earth,
Who share the author's thoughts;
And if there are, well, let them write—
Care of the publishers;
Some portion of the wreckage may be salvaged
    ere we go.
Call it, then, Public Relations.
But, finally, it is a last salute,
A way of saying goodnight.
And because of this, in this late evening of our
    dying world,
I'm going to end by quoting *in extenso*
Possibly the loveliest evening poem ever penned.
It's Collins's

Ode to Evening.

If aught of oaten stop or pastoral song

May hope, chaste Eve, to soothe thy modest ear
   Like thy own solemn springs,
   Thy springs, and dying gales;

O Nymph reserved,—while now the bright-hair'd
   sun
Sits in yon western tent, whose cloudy skirts,
   With brede ethereal wove,
   O'erhang his wavy bed,

Now air is hush'd, save where the weak-eyed bat
With short shrill shriek flits by on leathern wing,
   Or where the beetle winds
   His small but sullen horn,

As oft he rises midst the twilight path
Against the pilgrim borne in heedless hum,—
   Now teach me, maid composed,
   To breathe some soften'd strain

Whose numbers, stealing through thy darkening vale,
May not unseemly with its stillness suit,
   As musing slow, I hail
   Thy genial loved return.

For when thy folding-star arising shows
His paly circlet, at his warning lamp
   The fragrant Hours and Elves
   Who slept in buds the day,

And many a Nymph who wreathes her brow with
      sedge
And sheds the freshening dew, and lovelier still,
   The pensive Pleasures sweet,
   Prepare thy shadowy car,

Then let me rove some wild and heathy scene,
Or find some ruin midst its dreary dells,
   Whose walls more awful nod
   By thy religious gleams.

Or if chill blustering winds or driving rain
Prevent my willing feet, be mine the hut
   That, from the mountain's side,
   Views wilds and swelling floods,

And hamlets brown, and dim-discover'd spires,
And hears their simple bell; and marks o'er all
   Thy dewy fingers draw
   The gradual dusky veil.

While Spring shall pour his showers, as oft he wont,
And bathe thy breathing tresses, meekest Eve!
   While Summer loves to sport
   Beneath thy lingering light;

While sallow Autumn fills thy lap with leaves;
Or Winter, yelling through the troublous air,
   Affrights thy shrinking train
   And rudely rends thy robes;

So long, regardful of thy quiet rule,
Shall Fancy, Friendship, Science, smiling Peace
    Thy gentlest influence own,
    And love thy favourite name!

That's poetry, that was.
And that too, once upon a time, was the world.
Goodbye, Goodbye, Beloved World.
I loved you dearly.